Learn JPA 2.0

Practical Guide

A. De Quattro

Practical Guide

1.Introduction to JPA 2.0

Java Persistence API (JPA) is a specification of the Java platform that provides robust and flexible data persistence management for Java applications. Persistence, in this context, refers to an application's ability to save the state of Java objects to a relational database and subsequently retrieve them. In other words, JPA handles the mapping between Java objects and relational database tables.

JPA was introduced to provide a standardized way of accessing and managing persistent data, offering a common interface for data management operations (CRUD: Create, Read, Update, Delete). It is part of the Java EE (Enterprise Edition) platform but can also be used in Java SE (Standard Edition) applications.

One of the primary features of JPA is the use of **entities**, which are specially annotated

Java classes that represent database tables. JPA allows developers to perform operations like creating, updating, deleting, and querying data in the database without having to write SQL queries directly, significantly simplifying the development and maintenance of applications.

The History and Development of JPA

The Origins of JPA

The need for effective persistence management in Java has been present since the early days of the language. Before JPA was introduced, developers used various techniques and frameworks to handle persistence, often with significant manual effort. One of the earliest approaches was the direct use of JDBC (Java Database Connectivity), an API that allows interaction with relational databases by executing SQL queries directly from Java code.

However, using JDBC presented some challenges. Writing SQL by hand and embedding it within Java code led to tight coupling with the database and code that was difficult to maintain and reuse. Additionally, the transition between Java's object-oriented model and the relational model of databases (known as **impedance mismatch**) required considerable effort.

To address these issues, various ORM (Object-Relational Mapping) frameworks were developed, such as Hibernate, which introduced a more abstract and object-oriented way to interact with databases. Hibernate, in particular, became very popular due to its ability to map Java objects to database tables without the need for SQL.

The Birth of JPA

In the late 1990s and early 2000s, the Java world saw a proliferation of ORM frameworks, each with its own features and peculiarities. However, the lack of a unified standard led to market fragmentation and interoperability issues between applications.

To address these needs, Sun Microsystems introduced JPA as part of the EJB 3.0 (Enterprise JavaBeans 3.0) specification in 2006, with Java EE 5. The goal was to provide a standardized solution for persistence management, integrating best practices from existing frameworks and simplifying the developer experience.

JPA was designed to be used in both enterprise and standalone contexts, making it a versatile choice for various types of Java applications. With its introduction, JPA quickly gained popularity due to its ability to abstract the complexity of data management while maintaining a high level of control and flexibility.

The Evolution of JPA

Since its first version, JPA has undergone several revisions and improvements to adapt to new needs and technologies. The JPA 2.0 version, released as part of Java EE 6 in 2009, represented a significant advancement, introducing numerous features and improvements over the original version.

JPA 2.0 introduced:

- **Criteria API**: A new way to build queries dynamically using Java rather than SQL. This approach allowed for constructing queries in a type-safe manner, reducing the risk of common errors and improving code maintainability.

- **Typed Queries**: Enhanced JPQL (Java Persistence Query Language) queries that now supported typing, improving code safety.

- **Secondary Cache**: Introduction of support for secondary caching, allowing greater efficiency in accessing previously read data.

- **Improvements in Mapping**: JPA 2.0

extended support for complex mappings, including elements such as collections, embedded objects, and maps.

These improvements made JPA an even more powerful and flexible tool for managing persistence, consolidating its adoption in both enterprise and agile modern environments.

Advantages of Using JPA

Adopting JPA in a project offers numerous benefits, reflecting in terms of productivity, code maintainability, efficiency, and portability.

1. Abstracting Persistence Complexity

One of JPA's main advantages is its ability to abstract much of the complexity associated with data persistence. With JPA, developers no longer need to write SQL code directly, reducing the possibility of errors and the need for in-depth knowledge of SQL and database structure. JPA automatically handles the generation of the SQL queries needed to perform CRUD operations, making the code more readable and maintainable.

2. Code Portability

JPA is a standardized specification, meaning that code written using JPA can run on any Java environment compatible with JPA. This reduces dependence on particular database vendors or ORM frameworks and facilitates migration of applications between different platforms and databases.

3. Reducing Impedance Mismatch

The concept of **impedance mismatch** refers to the conceptual differences between the object model of the programming language and the relational model of databases. JPA, through its ORM capabilities, helps reduce this mismatch by automatically mapping Java classes and attributes to database tables and columns. This makes developing object-oriented applications more intuitive and natural.

4. Enhanced Developer Productivity

With JPA, much of the manual work associated with persistence management is automated. Using Java entities to represent database tables allows developers to work directly with Java objects, reducing the time needed to implement persistence and focusing more on business logic.

Additionally, JPA provides tools and features such as the Criteria API that simplify writing complex queries programmatically, further enhancing productivity.

5. Easier Code Maintenance

The separation between the business model and the persistence layer allows for easier and safer code maintenance. Changes to the database, such as adding or removing columns, can be managed without significantly affecting the rest of the application, thanks to JPA's flexibility in mapping objects.

Moreover, with the use of annotations and XML mapping files, JPA makes it easier to document and maintain the correspondence between the object model and the database model.

6. Support for Transactions and Concurrency

JPA provides robust support for transaction management, which is crucial for ensuring data consistency and integrity. This is particularly important in applications that need to handle complex operations involving multiple entities or ensure the atomicity of operations.

Furthermore, JPA effectively manages concurrency, offering various transaction isolation levels and mechanisms for handling concurrency conflicts, such as entity versioning.

7. Caching and Performance

JPA includes caching mechanisms that significantly enhance application performance. The first-level cache (transaction-level cache) is automatically managed by the EntityManager and ensures that the same entities are not loaded multiple times during a single transaction. The optional second-level cache allows entities to be kept in memory even beyond the transaction duration, further reducing the number of database accesses and improving overall performance.

8. Community and Support

As an official Java standard, JPA benefits from a vast ecosystem of tools, libraries, and frameworks that extend its capabilities. Additionally, being supported by a large and active community makes it easy to find resources, documentation, examples, and assistance for any issues related to using JPA.

JPA 2.0 represents a significant step forward in Java persistence management, providing a standard and robust interface for interacting with relational databases. Its ability to abstract complexity, reduce impedance mismatch, enhance productivity, and facilitate code maintenance makes it an essential tool for modern Java application development.

By adopting JPA, developers can focus more on business logic, leaving persistence management to a reliable and flexible framework. With these characteristics, JPA continues to be one of the most widely used and appreciated technologies in the Java community, establishing itself as the de facto standard for object persistence management in both enterprise and non-enterprise environments.

2. Fundamental Concepts of JPA 2.0

Entity and Managed Persistence Context

What is an Entity?

In the context of JPA (Java Persistence API), an **entity** is a Java class that represents a table in a relational database. Each instance of an entity corresponds to a row in the table. Entities are the foundation of the data model in a JPA application and are defined by a Java class annotated with `@Entity`. These classes contain attributes that directly map to the columns of the table.

Here is an example of an entity:

```java

import javax.persistence.Entity;

import javax.persistence.Id;
```

```
@Entity
public class User {

   @Id
   private Long id;

   private String username;
   private String password;

   // Constructors, getters, and setters
   public User() {}

   public User(Long id, String username,
String password) {
      this.id = id;
      this.username = username;
      this.password = password;
```

```
}

public Long getId() {
    return id;
}

public void setId(Long id) {
    this.id = id;
}

public String getUsername() {
    return username;
}

public void setUsername(String username)
{
    this.username = username;
}
```

```
    public String getPassword() {
        return password;
    }

    public void setPassword(String password) {
        this.password = password;
    }
}
```

In this example, the `User` class is annotated with `@Entity`, which indicates to JPA that this class should be managed as an entity. The `id` attribute is annotated with `@Id`, marking it as the primary key of the table.

Managed Persistence Context

The **persistence context** in JPA is an environment where entities are managed. When an entity is associated with a persistence context, it is considered **managed**, meaning that any changes made to the entity will automatically be synchronized with the database at the end of the transaction.

The persistence context is managed by an `EntityManager` object, which is responsible for operations such as creating, reading, updating, and deleting entities from the database.

Here is an example of how to use `EntityManager` to manage an entity:

```java
import javax.persistence.EntityManager;

import
javax.persistence.EntityManagerFactory;

import javax.persistence.Persistence;
```

```
public class UserService {

    private EntityManagerFactory
entityManagerFactory;

    public UserService() {
        entityManagerFactory =
Persistence.createEntityManagerFactory("exa
mple-unit");
    }

    public void createUser(Long id, String
username, String password) {
        EntityManager entityManager =
entityManagerFactory.createEntityManager();
        entityManager.getTransaction().begin();

        User user = new User(id, username,
password);
```

```
        entityManager.persist(user);  // The entity is managed by the persistence context



entityManager.getTransaction().commit();
        entityManager.close();
    }

    public User findUser(Long id) {
        EntityManager entityManager = entityManagerFactory.createEntityManager();
        User user = entityManager.find(User.class, id);
        entityManager.close();
        return user;
    }
}
```

In this example, the `EntityManager` manages the persistence context. When you call `persist`, the `User` object becomes managed, and its changes will be tracked by the persistence context until the transaction is closed.

Entity Lifecycle

Entities in JPA go through different states throughout their lifecycle. These states define how the entity interacts with the persistence context. The main states of an entity are:

1. **New (Transient)**: The entity has just been created but is not yet associated with the persistence context. It has no representation in the database.

2. **Managed**: The entity is associated with the persistence context and is being tracked by JPA. Any changes made to the entity will be synchronized with the database when the

transaction is completed.

3. **Detached**: The entity was associated with a persistence context but is now disconnected. It is no longer tracked by JPA but can be reattached later.

4. **Removed**: The entity is associated with the persistence context but has been marked for removal. It will be deleted from the database when the transaction is completed.

Example of Lifecycle Management

```java

import javax.persistence.EntityManager;

import javax.persistence.EntityManagerFactory;

import javax.persistence.Persistence;
```

```
public class LifecycleExample {

    public static void main(String[] args) {
        EntityManagerFactory
entityManagerFactory =
Persistence.createEntityManagerFactory("exa
mple-unit");
        EntityManager entityManager =
entityManagerFactory.createEntityManager();

        // New (Transient) state
        User user = new User(1L, "newUser",
"password123");

        entityManager.getTransaction().begin();

        // Managed state
        entityManager.persist(user);

        // Removed state
```

```
        entityManager.remove(user);

entityManager.getTransaction().commit();
        entityManager.close();

        // Detached state
        user.setPassword("newPassword");
        // Changes are not synchronized because the entity is in the Detached state
    }
}
```

In this example, a `User` entity goes through various states: from `New` when it is created, to `Managed` when it is passed to `persist`, and finally `Removed` when it is passed to `remove`.

Identifiers and Primary Keys

Each entity must have a unique identifier, which maps to the primary key of the table in the database. In JPA, identifiers are declared using the `@Id` annotation. Additionally, JPA offers various strategies for automatic identifier generation, such as `AUTO`, `SEQUENCE`, `TABLE`, and `IDENTITY`.

Example of Identifier with Automatic Generation

```java
import javax.persistence.Entity;

import javax.persistence.GeneratedValue;

import javax.persistence.GenerationType;

import javax.persistence.Id;


@Entity
```

```
public class Product {

    @Id
    @GeneratedValue(strategy =
GenerationType.AUTO)
    private Long id;

    private String name;
    private Double price;

    // Constructors, getters, and setters
    public Product() {}

    public Product(String name, Double price)
{
        this.name = name;
        this.price = price;
    }
```

```
public Long getId() {
    return id;
}

public void setId(Long id) {
    this.id = id;
}

public String getName() {
    return name;
}

public void setName(String name) {
    this.name = name;
}

public Double getPrice() {
    return price;
```

```
    }

    public void setPrice(Double price) {
        this.price = price;
    }
}
```

In this example, the `id` identifier is automatically generated using the `GenerationType.AUTO` strategy, which allows JPA to choose the best generation approach based on the underlying database.

Relationships between Entities

One of the strengths of JPA is its ability to map relationships between entities, reflecting the relationships that exist between tables in the database. Relationships can be of various types:

- **One-to-One**: An entity is associated with only one other entity.

- **One-to-Many**: An entity is associated with many other entities.

- **Many-to-One**: Many entities are associated with a single entity.

- **Many-to-Many**: Many entities are associated with many other entities.

One-to-One Relationships

A **One-to-One** relationship indicates that a row in one table is associated with a single row in another table. This relationship can be bidirectional or unidirectional.

Example of Unidirectional One-to-One Relationship

```java
```

```
import javax.persistence.Entity;
import javax.persistence.Id;
import javax.persistence.OneToOne;

@Entity
public class Address {

    @Id
    private Long id;

    private String street;
    private String city;

    @OneToOne
    private User user;

    // Constructors, getters, and setters
    public Address() {}
```

```
    public Address(Long id, String street,
String city, User user) {
        this.id = id;
        this.street = street;
        this.city = city;
        this.user = user;
    }

    public Long getId() {
        return id;
    }

    public void setId(Long id) {
        this.id = id;
    }

    public String getStreet() {
```

```
    return street;
}

public void setStreet(String street) {
    this.street = street;
}

public String getCity() {
    return city;
}

public void setCity(String city) {
    this.city = city;
}

public User getUser() {
    return user;
}
```

```
    public void setUser(User user) {
        this.user = user;
    }
}
```

In this example, the `Address` class has a One-to-One relationship with `User`. The mapping is unidirectional, so only `Address` knows about `User`.

One-to-Many Relationships

A **One-to-Many** relationship indicates that a row in one table is associated with multiple rows in another table. This type of relationship is commonly used, for example, in contexts where a customer can have multiple orders.

Example of Bidirectional One-to-Many Relationship

```java
import javax.persistence.*;
import java.util.List;

@Entity
public class Customer {

    @Id
    @GeneratedValue(strategy = GenerationType.AUTO)
    private Long id;

    private String name;

    @OneToMany(mappedBy = "customer")
    private List<Order> orders;
```

```
// Constructors, getters, and setters
public Customer() {}


public Customer(String name) {
    this.name = name;
}


public Long getId() {
    return id;
}


public void setId(Long id) {
    this.id = id;
}


public String getName() {
    return name;
```

```
    }

    public void setName(String name) {
        this.name = name;
    }

    public List<Order> getOrders() {
        return orders;
    }

    public void setOrders(List<Order> orders)
{
        this.orders = orders;
    }
}
```

```
@Entity
public class Order {

    @Id
    @GeneratedValue(strategy =
GenerationType.AUTO)
    private Long id;

    private String product;

    @ManyToOne
    @JoinColumn(name = "customer_id")
    private Customer customer;

    // Constructors, getters, and setters
    public Order() {}

    public Order(String product, Customer
customer) {
```

```
    this.product = product;
    this.customer = customer;
}

public Long getId() {
    return id;
}

public void setId(Long id) {
    this.id = id;
}

public String getProduct() {
    return product;
}

public void setProduct(String product) {
    this.product = product;
```

```
    }

    public Customer getCustomer() {
        return customer;
    }

    public void setCustomer(Customer customer) {
        this.customer = customer;
    }
}
```

In this example, `Customer` has a one-to-many relationship with `Order`, and `Order` has a many-to-one relationship with `Customer`. The relationship is bidirectional, meaning both entities are aware of each other.

Summary

Understanding the fundamentals of JPA, including how entities and their states work, the role of the persistence context, and how to map relationships between entities, is crucial for building robust and efficient data-driven Java applications. JPA abstracts much of the complexity of database interaction, allowing developers to focus on the business logic while maintaining control over the persistence layer.

3.Configuration of JPA 2.0

The Java Persistence API (JPA) is a Java framework that standardizes the mapping between Java objects and relational databases. This framework is part of the Java Enterprise Edition (Java EE) ecosystem and is primarily used to manage data persistence in Java applications. To use JPA in a project, it is necessary to correctly configure the persistence context. This configuration includes defining database connections, setting various properties, and integrating the required libraries into the project. In this guide, we will explore the details of configuring JPA 2.0, covering the `persistence.xml` file, Maven dependencies, and the use of different JPA implementations.

Configuring `persistence.xml`

The `persistence.xml` file is the heart of JPA configuration. It defines the persistence unit, which specifies how the JPA framework should behave for a particular set of classes and database tables. This file is usually located in the `META-INF` directory within the application's classpath.

Basic Structure of `persistence.xml`

The basic structure of the `persistence.xml` file is as follows:

```xml

<?xml version="1.0" encoding="UTF-8"?>

<persistence
xmlns="http://xmlns.jcp.org/xml/ns/persistenc
e"


xmlns:xsi="http://www.w3.org/2001/XMLSc
hema-instance"


xsi:schemaLocation="http://xmlns.jcp.org/xml
/ns/persistence
http://xmlns.jcp.org/xml/ns/persistence/persist
```

```
ence_2_0.xsd"
        version="2.0">

   <persistence-unit
name="myPersistenceUnit" transaction-
type="RESOURCE_LOCAL">

<provider>org.hibernate.jpa.HibernatePersiste
nceProvider</provider>

      <class>com.example.model.User</class>

<class>com.example.model.Product</class>

      <properties>
         <property
name="javax.persistence.jdbc.driver"
value="org.h2.Driver"/>
         <property
name="javax.persistence.jdbc.url"
```

```
value="jdbc:h2:mem:testdb"/>

        <property
name="javax.persistence.jdbc.user"
value="sa"/>

        <property
name="javax.persistence.jdbc.password"
value=""/>


        <property name="hibernate.dialect"
value="org.hibernate.dialect.H2Dialect"/>

        <property
name="hibernate.hbm2ddl.auto"
value="update"/>

        <property name="hibernate.show_sql"
value="true"/>

      </properties>

   </persistence-unit>


</persistence>
```

Let's look at the details of the main sections of this file:

1. **`<persistence>` Element**

The root element of the file is `<persistence>`, which contains one or more `<persistence-unit>` elements. The `<persistence>` element also includes some XML namespaces and attributes, including `xmlns`, `xsi:schemaLocation`, and `version`. The version in this case is `2.0`, indicating that this is a configuration for JPA 2.0.

2. **`<persistence-unit>` Element**

The `<persistence-unit>` element is the core of the configuration. It defines a single persistence unit, which is a group of persistent classes and their configurations. The `name` attribute of the `<persistence-unit>` element is mandatory and identifies the persistence unit. In this example, the persistence unit's name is `myPersistenceUnit`.

The `transaction-type` attribute can take two main values:

- `JTA` (Java Transaction API): Used in Java EE environments, where transaction management is delegated to the container.

- `RESOURCE_LOCAL`: Used in standalone or Java SE applications, where transactions are managed locally by the application.

3. **`<provider>` Element**

The `<provider>` element specifies the JPA implementation you want to use. In this example, `org.hibernate.jpa.HibernatePersistenceProvider` indicates that Hibernate is the JPA implementation in use. Other common implementations include EclipseLink (`org.eclipse.persistence.jpa.PersistenceProvider`) and Apache OpenJPA (`org.apache.openjpa.persistence.PersistenceP roviderImpl`).

4. **`<class>` Element**

The `<class>` elements list all the entity classes managed by this persistence unit. These classes must be annotated with `@Entity`. In this example, `User` and `Product` are two entities included in the persistence unit.

5. **`<properties>` Element**

The `<properties>` element contains configuration properties specific to the database and the chosen JPA implementation. Some common properties include:

- `javax.persistence.jdbc.driver`: The JDBC driver to use.

- `javax.persistence.jdbc.url`: The database

connection URL.

- `javax.persistence.jdbc.user`: The username for the database connection.

- `javax.persistence.jdbc.password`: The password for the database connection.

Additionally, there are provider-specific properties, such as those for Hibernate:

- `hibernate.dialect`: Specifies the SQL dialect of the database in use. In this case, `org.hibernate.dialect.H2Dialect` is used for the H2 database.

- `hibernate.hbm2ddl.auto`: Controls how Hibernate handles the database schema (common values are `validate`, `update`, `create`, `create-drop`).

- `hibernate.show_sql`: If set to `true`, Hibernate will show the generated SQL queries in the console.

Maven Dependencies for JPA

To use JPA in a Maven project, you need to include the appropriate dependencies in the `pom.xml` file. The dependencies vary depending on the chosen JPA implementation. Below, we will look at the dependencies for some of the most common JPA implementations.

1. **Hibernate**

Hibernate is one of the most popular JPA implementations. To use Hibernate with JPA 2.0, the `pom.xml` file must include the following dependencies:

```xml
<dependency>
   <groupId>org.hibernate</groupId>
   <artifactId>hibernate-core</artifactId>
   <version>5.4.33.Final</version>
</dependency>
```

```
<dependency>
   <groupId>org.hibernate</groupId>
   <artifactId>hibernate-entitymanager</artifactId>
   <version>5.4.33.Final</version>
</dependency>

<dependency>
   <groupId>javax.persistence</groupId>
   <artifactId>javax.persistence-api</artifactId>
   <version>2.2</version>
</dependency>

<dependency>
   <groupId>org.h2</groupId>
   <artifactId>h2</artifactId>
   <version>1.4.200</version>
```

<scope>runtime</scope>

</dependency>

```

- `hibernate-core`: The main Hibernate library, which includes the ORM mapping engine.

- `hibernate-entitymanager`: Hibernate extension for JPA, adding JPA-specific support.

- `javax.persistence-api`: The standard JPA API.

- `h2`: A lightweight in-memory SQL database used for examples and testing.

#### 2. **EclipseLink**

EclipseLink is the reference implementation for JPA. Maven dependencies for EclipseLink are:
```

```xml
<dependency>

<groupId>org.eclipse.persistence</groupId>
   <artifactId>eclipselink</artifactId>
   <version>2.7.7</version>
</dependency>

<dependency>
   <groupId>javax.persistence</groupId>
   <artifactId>javax.persistence-api</artifactId>
   <version>2.2</version>
</dependency>

<dependency>
   <groupId>org.h2</groupId>
   <artifactId>h2</artifactId>
   <version>1.4.200</version>
```

```
    <scope>runtime</scope>
</dependency>
```

- `eclipselink`: Includes the entire EclipseLink framework, the JPA implementation, and other advanced features.

- `javax.persistence-api`: The standard JPA API.

- `h2`: The database used for examples.

3. **Apache OpenJPA**

OpenJPA is another open-source JPA implementation. To use OpenJPA, the dependencies are:

```xml
<dependency>
    <groupId>org.apache.openjpa</groupId>
```

```xml
    <artifactId>openjpa</artifactId>
    <version>3.1.2</version>
</dependency>

<dependency>
    <groupId>javax.persistence</groupId>
    <artifactId>javax.persistence-api</artifactId>
    <version>2.2</version>
</dependency>

<dependency>
    <groupId>org.h2</groupId>
    <artifactId>h2</artifactId>
    <version>1.4.200</version>
    <scope>runtime</scope>
</dependency>
```

- `openjpa`: The main OpenJPA library.

- `javax.persistence-api`: The standard JPA API.

- `h2`: The database used for examples.

Using JPA with Different Implementations

JPA is a standard API and can be used with various implementations such as Hibernate, EclipseLink, and OpenJPA. The choice of implementation often depends on specific project requirements, development team preferences, or support for advanced features offered by each provider.

1. **Hibernate**

Hibernate is one of the most widely used JPA providers due to its large community, detailed documentation, and its ability to handle complex ORM mapping scenarios. Hibernate also offers a range of additional features beyond the standard JPA specification, such as support for advanced native SQL queries and second-level caching.

When using Hibernate as a JPA implementation, you benefit from:

- A robust and mature mapping engine.
- A wide range of dialects to support various databases.
- Advanced caching features to optimize performance.
- Integration with other technologies in the Spring stack.

To configure Hibernate, simply include the dependency in the `pom.xml` file and specify `org.hibernate.jpa.HibernatePersistenceProvider` as the `<provider>` in the `persistence.xml` file.

2. **EclipseLink**

EclipseLink is the reference implementation of JPA and is known for its performance and support for advanced features such as dynamic weaving, criteria API, and NoSQL integration. It is often used in enterprise projects, especially those running on Oracle or other large-scale databases.

Key features of EclipseLink include:

- Support for both relational and non-relational (NoSQL) databases.

- Advanced support for JPA 2.0 features, such as the criteria API.

- Integration with Oracle products, making it a

preferred choice for Oracle DB environments.

To use EclipseLink, ensure the `eclipselink` dependency is included in your `pom.xml` file and configure the `<provider>` as `org.eclipse.persistence.jpa.PersistenceProvider`.

3. **Apache OpenJPA**

OpenJPA is an Apache project that provides a flexible and extensible JPA implementation. It is known for its modular architecture and the ability to integrate with a wide range of database systems. OpenJPA is often chosen for projects that require a high degree of customization or integration with Apache projects.

Advantages of using OpenJPA include:

- Flexibility and extensibility due to its

modular architecture.

- Support for a wide range of databases.

- Integration with Apache projects like Geronimo and TomEE.

To configure OpenJPA, include the `openjpa` dependency in your `pom.xml` and set the `<provider>` as `org.apache.openjpa.persistence.PersistenceProviderImpl`.

JPA 2.0 is a powerful framework that simplifies database interactions in Java applications by abstracting the complexities of JDBC and SQL. Configuring JPA involves setting up the `persistence.xml` file, which defines the persistence unit and its properties, as well as including the necessary dependencies in your Maven project. Depending on your project needs, you can choose from several JPA implementations, such as Hibernate, EclipseLink, or Apache OpenJPA, each offering unique features and optimizations. Understanding these configurations and the role of each implementation will allow you to leverage JPA effectively in your projects.

4.Basic Operations with JPA 2.0

With JPA, developers can map Java objects to relational database tables, perform CRUD operations (Create, Read, Update, Delete), and define queries using the Java Persistence Query Language (JPQL) or the Criteria API. In this guide, we will explore the basic operations with JPA 2.0, focusing on creating an `EntityManager`, persisting, updating, removing, and retrieving entities, including the use of JPQL and the Criteria API.

Creating an EntityManager

The `EntityManager` is the main JPA interface for interacting with the persistence context, which manages the lifecycle of entities. The `EntityManager` is responsible for creating, reading, updating, and deleting entities in the database.

Basic Configuration

Before creating an `EntityManager`, you need to configure the persistence unit in the `persistence.xml` file as described in the previous section. Once the persistence unit is configured, you can create an `EntityManager` as follows:

```java
import javax.persistence.EntityManager;

import
javax.persistence.EntityManagerFactory;

import javax.persistence.Persistence;


public class Main {


    public static void main(String[] args) {

        // Create an EntityManagerFactory using
the persistence unit defined in persistence.xml

        EntityManagerFactory emf =
Persistence.createEntityManagerFactory("my
PersistenceUnit");
```

```
// Create an EntityManager
EntityManager em =
emf.createEntityManager();

// Begin a transaction
em.getTransaction().begin();

// Persistence operations here...

// Commit the transaction
em.getTransaction().commit();

// Close the EntityManager
em.close();

// Close the EntityManagerFactory
emf.close();
```

    }

}

```

#### Code Explanation

1. **EntityManagerFactory**: An `EntityManagerFactory` is created using the persistence unit defined in the `persistence.xml` file. This object is expensive to create, so it is typically shared across multiple `EntityManager` instances.

2. **EntityManager**: Using the `EntityManagerFactory`, an `EntityManager` is created. This object is thread-unsafe, so it should not be shared between multiple threads.

3. **Transactions**: Persistence operations must be executed within a transaction. Here, we use `em.getTransaction().begin()` to start a
```

transaction and `em.getTransaction().commit()` to commit the transaction.

4. **Resource Closure**: After use, the `EntityManager` and `EntityManagerFactory` must be closed to free up resources.

Persisting Entities

Persisting an entity involves saving the entity to the database. In JPA, this is done through the `persist()` method of the `EntityManager`.

Creating and Persisting a New Entity

Let's assume we have a `User` entity:

```java

import javax.persistence.Entity;
```

```
import javax.persistence.GeneratedValue;
import javax.persistence.GenerationType;
import javax.persistence.Id;

@Entity
public class User {

    @Id
    @GeneratedValue(strategy =
GenerationType.AUTO)
    private Long id;

    private String username;
    private String email;

    // Constructors, getters, and setters
    public User() {}
```

```
    public User(String username, String email)
{
        this.username = username;
        this.email = email;
    }

    public Long getId() {
        return id;
    }

    public void setId(Long id) {
        this.id = id;
    }

    public String getUsername() {
        return username;
    }
```

```
  public void setUsername(String username) {
    this.username = username;
  }

  public String getEmail() {
    return email;
  }

  public void setEmail(String email) {
    this.email = email;
  }
}
```

To save a new `User` entity to the database, we can use the following code:

```java
```

```
public class Main {

   public static void main(String[] args) {
       EntityManagerFactory emf =
Persistence.createEntityManagerFactory("my
PersistenceUnit");
       EntityManager em =
emf.createEntityManager();

       // Create a new User
       User newUser = new User("john_doe",
"john.doe@example.com");

       em.getTransaction().begin();

       // Persist the User entity
       em.persist(newUser);

       em.getTransaction().commit();
```

```
        em.close();
        emf.close();
    }
}
```

Code Explanation

1. **Entity Creation**: We create a new instance of the `User` class.

2. **Entity Persistence**: We use `em.persist(newUser)` to save the `newUser` object to the database. After committing the transaction, the object is inserted as a new row in the corresponding table.

Entity State

In JPA, an entity can be in one of the

following states:

- **New/Transient**: The entity has just been created but is not yet associated with a persistence context.

- **Managed**: The entity is associated with a persistence context and is synchronized with the database.

- **Detached**: The entity was in a `Managed` state but is no longer associated with a persistence context.

- **Removed**: The entity is marked for removal from the database.

Updating Entities

Updating an entity in JPA involves modifying the fields of the managed entity and committing the transaction.

Update Example

Let's imagine we want to update the email of an existing `User` in the database:

```java
public class Main {

    public static void main(String[] args) {
        EntityManagerFactory emf =
Persistence.createEntityManagerFactory("my
PersistenceUnit");
        EntityManager em =
emf.createEntityManager();

        em.getTransaction().begin();

        // Retrieve the existing User entity
        User existingUser = em.find(User.class,
1L);

        if (existingUser != null) {
```

```
        // Update the email

existingUser.setEmail("new.email@example.com");
      }

      em.getTransaction().commit();

      em.close();
      emf.close();
   }
}
```

Code Explanation

1. **Entity Retrieval**: We use `em.find()` to retrieve the existing `User` entity with an `id` of `1L`. This object is now in a `Managed` state.

2. **Entity Update**: We modify the email using the `setEmail()` method.

3. **Committing Changes**: After committing the transaction, the changes are propagated to the database.

Removing Entities

Removing an entity in JPA involves deleting the corresponding row from the database. This can be done using the `remove()` method of the `EntityManager`.

Removal Example

Suppose we want to remove a `User` with a specific `id` from the database:

```java
public class Main {

    public static void main(String[] args) {
        EntityManagerFactory emf = Persistence.createEntityManagerFactory("myPersistenceUnit");
        EntityManager em = emf.createEntityManager();

        em.getTransaction().begin();

        // Retrieve the existing User entity
        User userToDelete = em.find(User.class, 1L);

        if (userToDelete != null) {
            // Remove the User entity
            em.remove(userToDelete);
```

```
        }

        em.getTransaction().commit();

        em.close();
        emf.close();
    }
}
```

Code Explanation

1. **Entity Retrieval**: We find the `User` entity that we want to remove.

2. **Entity Removal**: We call `em.remove()` passing the `userToDelete` object. This marks the entity for removal.

3. **Commit the Removal**: After committing the transaction, the entity is effectively deleted from the database.

Retrieving Entities

Retrieving entities in JPA can be done in various ways, using JPQL queries, the Criteria API, or simple find methods like `find()`.

Using JPQL

JPQL (Java Persistence Query Language) is a query language similar to SQL but operates on entities rather than database tables. JPQL allows you to execute queries that select, update, or delete entities.

JPQL Query Example

Imagine we want to find all users with a

specific username:

```java
import javax.persistence.TypedQuery;
import java.util.List;

public class Main {

    public static void main(String[] args) {
        EntityManagerFactory emf = Persistence.createEntityManagerFactory("myPersistenceUnit");
        EntityManager em = emf.createEntityManager();

        em.getTransaction().begin();

        // Create the JPQL query
        String jpql = "SELECT u FROM User u
```

```
WHERE u.username = :username";
        TypedQuery<User> query =
em.createQuery(jpql, User.class);
        query.setParameter("username",
"john_doe");


        // Execute the query and retrieve the
results
        List<User> users =
query.getResultList();


        for (User user : users) {
            System.out.println(user.getUsername()
+ ": " + user.getEmail());
        }


        em.getTransaction().commit();


        em.close();
        emf.close();
```

```
    }
}
```

Code Explanation

1. **Query Creation**: We define a JPQL string to select all `User` entities with a specific username.

2. **Parameter Setting**: We use `query.setParameter()` to replace the `:username` parameter with the desired value.

3. **Executing the Query**: We execute the query with `getResultList()` to obtain a list of matching results.

Criteria API Queries

JPA 2.0's Criteria API allows you to construct queries programmatically. This is particularly useful for creating dynamic queries.

Criteria API Query Example

Suppose we want to retrieve all users with an email ending with a specific domain:

```java
import javax.persistence.criteria.CriteriaBuilder;
import javax.persistence.criteria.CriteriaQuery;
import javax.persistence.criteria.Root;

public class Main {

  public static void main(String[] args) {
    EntityManagerFactory emf =
```

```
Persistence.createEntityManagerFactory("my
PersistenceUnit");
        EntityManager em = emf


.createEntityManager();


        em.getTransaction().begin();


        // Get the CriteriaBuilder
        CriteriaBuilder cb =
em.getCriteriaBuilder();


        // Create a CriteriaQuery object
        CriteriaQuery<User> cq =
cb.createQuery(User.class);


        // Define a root of the query
        Root<User> root = cq.from(User.class);
```

```
    // Define the query

cq.select(root).where(cb.like(root.get("email")
, "%@example.com"));


    // Execute the query

    List<User> users =
em.createQuery(cq).getResultList();


    for (User user : users) {

        System.out.println(user.getUsername()
+ ": " + user.getEmail());

    }


    em.getTransaction().commit();


    em.close();

    emf.close();

  }
```

}

```

##### Code Explanation

1. **CriteriaBuilder**: We obtain a `CriteriaBuilder` instance from the `EntityManager`.

2. **CriteriaQuery**: We create a `CriteriaQuery` object specifying the result type (`User`).

3. **Root**: We define the root of the query (i.e., the entity to be queried).

4. **Query Construction**: We construct the query using the Criteria API's fluent API.

5. **Executing the Query**: We execute the
```

query similarly to how we did with JPQL.

This guide provided an overview of basic JPA operations, including creating an `EntityManager`, persisting, updating, removing, and retrieving entities using JPQL and the Criteria API. JPA simplifies database interactions by abstracting much of the complexity involved in managing database access in a Java application. By mastering these basic operations, you can effectively manage entity data in your Java applications.

5.Transaction Management with JPA 2.0

Transaction management is a fundamental aspect of data persistence and concurrency control in Java applications. In JPA 2.0, transactions are essential to ensure that database operations are performed safely and consistently. Transactions ensure that a set of database operations is either completed successfully as a single unit of work or, in the event of an error, that none of the operations are applied, restoring the database to its previous state.

In this guide, we will explore transaction concepts in JPA 2.0, transaction management through the `EntityManager`, and support for both local transactions and JTA (Java Transaction API).

1. **Transaction Definition**

A transaction is a sequence of database

operations that are executed as a single unit of work. Transactions have the following properties, known as ACID:

- **Atomicity**: The transaction is indivisible; either all operations are executed successfully, or none are executed.

- **Consistency**: The transaction takes the database from one consistent state to another consistent state.

- **Isolation**: Concurrent transactions are executed in such a way that no transaction interferes with another. The effects of a transaction are not visible to other transactions until it is committed.

- **Durability**: Once a transaction has been committed, the changes are permanent and cannot be undone, even in the event of a system failure.

2. **Transaction States**

Transactions can be in one of the following

states:

- **Started**: The transaction has been initiated but not yet committed or rolled back.

- **Completed**: The transaction has been successfully committed, and all changes have been saved to the database.

- **Rolled Back**: The transaction has been rolled back, and all changes have been reverted to their previous state.

3. **Transaction Management**

Transactions must be properly managed to maintain database consistency and integrity. In JPA, transaction management can be handled either programmatically through the `EntityManager` API or declaratively using JTA (Java Transaction API) in enterprise application contexts.

Transaction Management with EntityManager

The `EntityManager` in JPA provides methods for managing transactions. Transaction management with the `EntityManager` is relatively simple and revolves around three main methods: `begin()`, `commit()`, and `rollback()`.

1. **Starting a Transaction**

A transaction is started using the `begin()` method of the `EntityTransaction`, which can be obtained through `EntityManager.getTransaction()`.

```java

import javax.persistence.EntityManager;

import
javax.persistence.EntityManagerFactory;

import javax.persistence.EntityTransaction;

import javax.persistence.Persistence;
```

```
public class TransactionExample {

    public static void main(String[] args) {
        EntityManagerFactory emf =
Persistence.createEntityManagerFactory("my
PersistenceUnit");
        EntityManager em =
emf.createEntityManager();

        EntityTransaction tx =
em.getTransaction();

        try {
            tx.begin();  // Start the transaction

            // Database operations here

            tx.commit(); // Commit the changes
```

```
        } catch (Exception e) {
            if (tx.isActive()) {
                tx.rollback(); // Rollback changes in case of an error
            }
            e.printStackTrace();
        } finally {
            em.close();  // Close the EntityManager
            emf.close(); // Close the EntityManagerFactory
        }
    }
}
```

2. **Completing the Transaction**

The `commit()` method applies all changes

made during the transaction to the database. Once `commit()` is called, the changes are permanent.

3. **Rolling Back the Transaction**

In case of an error, the `rollback()` method can be called to undo all changes made during the transaction. This restores the database to the state it was in before the transaction began.

Support for Local Transactions and JTA

JPA supports both local transactions and JTA-managed transactions. The choice between the two depends on the context in which JPA is being used.

1. **Local Transactions**

Local transactions are managed directly

within the `EntityManager`. This is typical in standalone applications or contexts not managed by an application server.

- **Configuration**: Local transactions are managed using `EntityTransaction`, as shown in the examples above.

- **Scope of Use**: Used in environments that do not require distributed transactional support or are not managed by an application server.

Local Transactions Example

```java

import javax.persistence.EntityManager;

import javax.persistence.EntityManagerFactory;

import javax.persistence.EntityTransaction;

import javax.persistence.Persistence;
```

```
public class LocalTransactionExample {

    public static void main(String[] args) {
        EntityManagerFactory emf =
Persistence.createEntityManagerFactory("my
PersistenceUnit");
        EntityManager em =
emf.createEntityManager();

        EntityTransaction tx =
em.getTransaction();

        try {
            tx.begin();  // Start the transaction

            // Create and persist a new entity
            User newUser = new User("alice",
"alice@example.com");
            em.persist(newUser);
```

```
            tx.commit(); // Commit the changes


        } catch (Exception e) {
            if (tx.isActive()) {
                tx.rollback(); // Rollback changes in case of an error
            }
            e.printStackTrace();
        } finally {
            em.close();  // Close the EntityManager
            emf.close(); // Close the EntityManagerFactory
        }
    }
}
```

2. **JTA (Java Transaction API)

Transactions**

JTA is used to manage transactions in enterprise environments, such as Java EE application servers, where transactions may involve multiple resources (databases, messaging systems, etc.). With JTA, transaction management is delegated to the container, which coordinates distributed transactions.

- **Configuration**: In a JTA environment, the `EntityManager` is container-managed, and transactions are managed through a `UserTransaction` or the container's transaction context.

- **Scope of Use**: Used in enterprise application contexts requiring distributed transaction management.

JTA Transactions Example

In an environment managed by an application

server, it is not necessary to manage transactions directly with `EntityTransaction`. Transaction management is delegated to the container. For example, in a Java EE application, the transaction can be managed through the container's transaction context.

```java
import javax.ejb.Stateless;

import javax.persistence.EntityManager;

import javax.persistence.PersistenceContext;

import javax.transaction.UserTransaction;

import javax.transaction.Transactional;


@Stateless

public class UserService {


    @PersistenceContext

    private EntityManager em;
```

```
@Resource
private UserTransaction utx;


@Transactional
public void createUser(User user) {
    try {
        utx.begin();  // Start the transaction
        em.persist(user);
        utx.commit(); // Commit the changes
    } catch (Exception e) {
        try {
            if (utx.getStatus() ==
Status.STATUS_ACTIVE) {
                utx.rollback(); // Rollback
changes in case of an error
            }
        } catch (Exception ex) {
            ex.printStackTrace();
        }
```

```
            e.printStackTrace();
        }
    }
}
```

Code Explanation

1. **@Stateless**: The `UserService` class is a stateless EJB (Enterprise JavaBean), managed by the container.

2. **@PersistenceContext**: The `EntityManager` is injected by the container.

3. **UserTransaction**: The `UserTransaction` is injected by the container and is used to start and manage transactions.

4. **@Transactional**: The `createUser`

method is annotated with `@Transactional`, which indicates that the container should automatically manage the transaction.

Advanced Considerations

1. **Concurrency Management**

JPA provides different strategies for concurrency management to ensure data consistency in multi-user environments. The two main strategies are:

- **Optimistic**: Uses a timestamp or version number to detect concurrency conflicts. Transactions that attempt to update data modified by another transaction will be blocked or rejected.
- **Pessimistic**: Locks records at the database level to prevent other users from modifying data during the transaction.

2. **Distributed Transactions**

In complex environments, it may be necessary to manage transactions that involve multiple resources. JTA and distributed transaction coordination APIs (such as XA Transactions) are used to handle such scenarios.

3. **Automatic Rollback and Exception Handling**

In transaction management scenarios, proper exception handling is crucial. Transactions should be automatically rolled back if an unhandled exception occurs, and resources should always be released in the event of an error.

Transaction management is a fundamental aspect of data persistence in JPA. Understanding how to start, commit, and roll back transactions, and knowing when to use local transactions or JTA, is essential for ensuring database consistency and integrity. In enterprise environments, managing distributed transactions becomes critical, and using JTA and distributed transactions ensures that operations across multiple resources are performed safely and coordinated.

Knowing how to manage transactions in JPA not only helps maintain data quality but also improves the robustness and scalability of Java applications, ensuring that database operations are performed reliably and securely.

6.Filters and Callbacks in JPA 2.0

Java Persistence API (JPA) 2.0 offers a wide range of tools to customize and manage data persistence. Among these tools are **listeners** and **callbacks**, which allow you to intercept events in the lifecycle of entities, and **query filters**, which enable dynamic filtering of queries. These mechanisms provide fine-grained control over how and when persistence operations are executed, enhancing the efficiency and flexibility of applications.

In this guide, we will explore the concepts of **Entity Listeners**, **Lifecycle Callbacks**, and **Query Filters**, providing details and practical examples for each.

Entity Listeners

Entity Listeners are classes containing

methods that handle specific events in the lifecycle of entities. These events include operations such as creating, modifying, and removing entities. Entity Listeners offer a way to apply cross-cutting logic that needs to be executed whenever an entity is persisted, updated, or removed.

1. **Defining an Entity Listener**

To define an Entity Listener, you need to create a separate class with methods annotated with JPA's lifecycle annotations. Each method in an Entity Listener must be annotated with one of the lifecycle annotations, such as `@PostPersist`, `@PostUpdate`, `@PostRemove`, `@PrePersist`, `@PreUpdate`, or `@PreRemove`.

Example of an Entity Listener

Suppose we have a `User` entity and want to track when a user is created or modified. We can create an Entity Listener to handle these events.

```java
import javax.persistence.PostPersist;
import javax.persistence.PostRemove;
import javax.persistence.PostUpdate;
import javax.persistence.PrePersist;
import javax.persistence.PreRemove;
import javax.persistence.PreUpdate;
import javax.persistence.Entity;
import javax.persistence.Id;
import javax.persistence.EntityListeners;

@Entity
@EntityListeners(UserListener.class)
public class User {
```

```
    @Id
    private Long id;
    private String username;
    private String email;

    // Constructors, getters, and setters
    public User() {}

    public User(Long id, String username,
String email) {
        this.id = id;
        this.username = username;
        this.email = email;
    }

    // Getters and setters
}
```

Now, let's create the `UserListener` class:

```java
import javax.persistence.PostPersist;
import javax.persistence.PostRemove;
import javax.persistence.PostUpdate;

public class UserListener {

    @PostPersist
    public void postPersist(User user) {
        System.out.println("User created: " +
user.getUsername());
    }

    @PostUpdate
    public void postUpdate(User user) {
```

```
        System.out.println("User updated: " + user.getUsername());
    }

    @PostRemove
    public void postRemove(User user) {
        System.out.println("User removed: " + user.getUsername());
    }
}
```

Code Explanation

1. **Lifecycle Annotations**: The `postPersist`, `postUpdate`, and `postRemove` methods are annotated with `@PostPersist`, `@PostUpdate`, and `@PostRemove`, respectively. These methods will be automatically called by JPA after persistence, update, and removal operations.

2. **Registering the Listener**: The `UserListener` class is registered as a listener for the `User` entity using the `@EntityListeners` annotation on the entity class.

Lifecycle Callbacks

Lifecycle Callbacks are methods defined within the entity itself and are annotated with the same annotations used for Entity Listener methods. These methods allow handling events in the entity's lifecycle directly within its class.

1. **Defining Lifecycle Callbacks**

Lifecycle Callbacks are methods that are automatically invoked by JPA when certain events occur in the entity's lifecycle.

Example of Lifecycle Callbacks

Let's modify the `User` entity to include Lifecycle Callbacks directly within the entity class:

```java
import javax.persistence.Entity;

import javax.persistence.Id;

import javax.persistence.PostPersist;

import javax.persistence.PostRemove;

import javax.persistence.PostUpdate;

import javax.persistence.PrePersist;

import javax.persistence.PreRemove;

import javax.persistence.PreUpdate;

@Entity

public class User {
```

```
    @Id
    private Long id;
    private String username;
    private String email;

    // Constructors, getters, and setters
    public User() {}

    public User(Long id, String username,
String email) {
        this.id = id;
        this.username = username;
        this.email = email;
    }

    @PrePersist
    public void prePersist() {
        System.out.println("Preparing to create
user: " + this.username);
```

```
    }

    @PostPersist
    public void postPersist() {
        System.out.println("User created: " +
this.username);
    }

    @PreUpdate
    public void preUpdate() {
        System.out.println("Preparing to update
user: " + this.username);
    }

    @PostUpdate
    public void postUpdate() {
        System.out.println("User updated: " +
this.username);
    }
```

```
    @PreRemove
    public void preRemove() {
        System.out.println("Preparing to remove user: " + this.username);
    }

    @PostRemove
    public void postRemove() {
        System.out.println("User removed: " + this.username);
    }
}
```

Code Explanation

1. **Lifecycle Annotations**: The `prePersist`, `postPersist`, `preUpdate`,

`postUpdate`, `preRemove`, and `postRemove` methods are annotated with `@PrePersist`, `@PostPersist`, `@PreUpdate`, `@PostUpdate`, `@PreRemove`, and `@PostRemove`, respectively. These methods will be automatically called by JPA at the respective points in the entity's lifecycle.

2. **Handling Events**: The Lifecycle Callback methods provide a way to handle events such as preparing for the creation, updating, and removal of the entity directly within the entity class.

Query Filters

Query Filters are used to apply dynamic filters to queries executed with JPA. Filters allow you to add conditions at the query level without having to modify the query code directly, making it easier to manage complex queries and separate filtering logic.

1. **Defining a Query Filter**

Query Filters are defined using the `@Filter` annotation and are associated with a query via the `@FilterDef` annotation. A filter can be applied at the entity level or a specific query level.

Example of a Query Filter

Suppose we have a `Product` entity and want to apply a filter to display only products that are available in stock. We define the filter as follows:

```java

import javax.persistence.Entity;

import javax.persistence.Id;

import javax.persistence.Column;

import javax.persistence.Table;
```

```
import org.hibernate.annotations.Filter;
import org.hibernate.annotations.FilterDef;
import org.hibernate.annotations.ParamDef;


@Entity
@Table(name = "products")
@FilterDef(name = "availableProducts",
parameters = @ParamDef(name = "inStock",
type = "boolean"))
@Filter(name = "availableProducts",
condition = "in_stock = :inStock")
public class Product {

    @Id
    private Long id;

    @Column(name = "name")
    private String name;
```

```
    @Column(name = "in_stock")
    private boolean inStock;

    // Constructors, getters, and setters
    public Product() {}

    public Product(Long id, String name, boolean inStock) {
        this.id = id;
        this.name = name;
        this.inStock = inStock;
    }

    // Getters and setters
}
```

Applying the Filter in the Query

To apply the filter to the query, we use the Hibernate API to set the filter parameters and apply it:

```java
import javax.persistence.EntityManager;

import
javax.persistence.EntityManagerFactory;

import javax.persistence.Persistence;

import javax.persistence.Query;

import org.hibernate.Session;

import org.hibernate.SessionFactory;

import org.hibernate.Transaction;


public class QueryFilterExample {


    public static void main(String[] args) {

        EntityManagerFactory emf =
Persistence.createEntityManagerFactory("my
PersistenceUnit");
```

```
    EntityManager em =
emf.createEntityManager();

    Session session =
em.unwrap(Session.class);

    // Apply the filter

session.enableFilter("availableProducts").setP
arameter("inStock", true);

    // Execute the query
    String hql = "FROM Product";
    Query query = session.createQuery(hql);
    List<Product> availableProducts =
query.getResultList();

    for (Product product : availableProducts)
{
```

```
System.out.println(product.getName());
        }



session.disableFilter("availableProducts");
        em.close();
        emf.close();
    }
}
```

Code Explanation

1. **Defining the Filter**: The `@FilterDef` annotation defines the filter and its parameters. The `@Filter` annotation applies the filter to the `Product` entity and specifies the query condition.

2. **Enabling the Filter**: We use

`session.enableFilter("availableProducts")` to enable the filter and set the `inStock` parameter.

3. **Executing the Query**: The query is executed as usual, but only the results that satisfy the filter are returned.

4. **Disabling the Filter**: After executing the query, the filter is disabled with `session.disableFilter("availableProducts")`.

Advanced Considerations

1. **Entity Listeners and Performance**

The use of Entity Listeners can impact performance, as each persistence operation involves executing the listener methods. It's important to evaluate the performance impact and use Entity Listeners only for logic that must be applied across all entities.

2. **Lifecycle Callbacks and Maintainability**

Lifecycle Callbacks are useful for encapsulating logic that needs to be executed at specific points in the entity's lifecycle. However, excessive use of Lifecycle Callbacks within entities can make the code difficult to maintain and understand. It's advisable to keep Lifecycle Callbacks simple and well-documented

.

3. **Query Filters and Complexity**

Query Filters offer great flexibility in managing queries but can add complexity to the code. It's important to plan and test filters to ensure they are applied correctly and do not negatively impact query performance.

Entity Listeners, **Lifecycle Callbacks**, and **Query Filters** are powerful tools offered by JPA 2.0 to manage data persistence in a more refined and controlled manner. Entity Listeners and Lifecycle Callbacks allow specific logic to be executed at precise points in the entity lifecycle, while Query Filters enable the application of dynamic conditions to queries. By using these tools appropriately, you can improve the robustness, maintainability, and flexibility of Java applications that use JPA, while ensuring accurate control over persistence operations and the data being managed.

7.Performance Optimization

When working with databases and data persistence, it is crucial to ensure that operations are executed efficiently to enhance the responsiveness and overall effectiveness of the application. The main optimization techniques include **Lazy** and **Eager Loading**, **Entity Caching**, and **Batch Processing**. In this guide, we will explore each of these aspects in detail, providing practical examples and in-depth explanations.

Lazy and Eager Loading

Lazy Loading and **Eager Loading** are two fundamental strategies for managing the loading of relationships between entities in JPA. These strategies directly impact the performance of queries and memory usage.

1. **Lazy Loading**

Lazy Loading is a strategy where associated data with an entity is not immediately loaded from the database. Instead, the data is only loaded when it is actually requested. This strategy can improve performance by avoiding the loading of unnecessary data, but it can also lead to performance issues if not managed properly.

Example of Lazy Loading

Let's consider two entities, `Author` and `Book`, where an author can have multiple books.

```java

import javax.persistence.Entity;

import javax.persistence.Id;

import javax.persistence.OneToMany;

import java.util.Set;
```

```
@Entity
public class Author {

    @Id
    private Long id;
    private String name;

    @OneToMany(mappedBy = "author")
    private Set<Book> books;

    // Constructors, getters, and setters
}
```

```java
import javax.persistence.Entity;
import javax.persistence.Id;
import javax.persistence.ManyToOne;
```

```
@Entity
public class Book {

    @Id
    private Long id;
    private String title;

    @ManyToOne
    private Author author;

    // Constructors, getters, and setters
}
```

In the code above, the relationship between `Author` and `Book` is defined as `@OneToMany` and `@ManyToOne`. By default, JPA uses Lazy Loading for collections, meaning that books will not be loaded when we load an author, but only when we access the `books` collection.

Using Lazy Loading

```java
EntityManager em = emf.createEntityManager();
Author author = em.find(Author.class, 1L); // Loads the author
Set<Book> books = author.getBooks(); // Books are not loaded yet
// Books are loaded only when we access the collection
```

Lazy Loading Issues

Lazy Loading can cause issues known as the

N+1 Select Problem, where one query to load an entity triggers additional queries to load the relationships. This can be avoided using techniques like batch fetching.

2. **Eager Loading**

Eager Loading is a strategy where all associated data with an entity is loaded immediately from the database when the main entity is loaded. This strategy is useful when it's certain that the associated data will be needed and can reduce the number of executed queries.

Example of Eager Loading

To enforce eager loading, use the `fetch` annotation with `FetchType.EAGER`:

```java
```

```
import javax.persistence.FetchType;
import javax.persistence.OneToMany;

@Entity
public class Author {

    @Id
    private Long id;
    private String name;

    @OneToMany(mappedBy = "author", fetch = FetchType.EAGER)
    private Set<Book> books;

    // Constructors, getters, and setters
}
```

Using Eager Loading

```java
EntityManager em =
emf.createEntityManager();
Author author = em.find(Author.class, 1L); //
Loads the author and associated books
immediately
Set<Book> books = author.getBooks(); //
Books are already loaded
```

Eager Loading Considerations

Although Eager Loading reduces the number of queries, it can increase the amount of data loaded into memory and the initial load time. It’s important to use it cautiously and only when truly necessary.

Entity Caching

Entity Caching is a fundamental technique to improve the performance of persistence operations. JPA offers various caching strategies to store data and reduce the number of database queries.

1. **First-Level Caching**

First-Level Caching is automatically managed by JPA and is based on the persistence context (EntityManager). Each `EntityManager` has an internal cache that stores entities retrieved during the current session. This means that if you request an entity multiple times during the same session, JPA will not execute repeated queries to the database.

Example of First-Level Caching

```java
```

EntityManager em =
emf.createEntityManager();

User user1 = em.find(User.class, 1L); // First query to the database

User user2 = em.find(User.class, 1L); // Retrieved from first-level cache, no query

```

#### 2. **Second-Level Caching**

**Second-Level Caching** is managed by the persistence provider and extends outside the persistence context. This type of caching stores entities at the session level of `EntityManagerFactory`, allowing entities to be reused across different sessions.

##### Configuring Second-Level Caching

To enable second-level caching, you need to configure the persistence provider (e.g.,
```

Hibernate) and annotate the entities with `@Cacheable` and `@Cache`.

```java
import org.hibernate.annotations.Cache;
import org.hibernate.annotations.CacheConcurrencyStrategy;

@Entity
@Cacheable
@Cache(usage = CacheConcurrencyStrategy.READ_WRITE)
public class User {

    @Id
    private Long id;
    private String name;
```

```
    // Constructors, getters, and setters
}
```

Configuring Hibernate for Second-Level Caching

In `persistence.xml` or `hibernate.cfg.xml`, enable second-level caching:

```xml
<property name="hibernate.cache.use_second_level_cache">true</property>
<property name="hibernate.cache.region.factory_class">org.hibernate.cache.ehcache.EhCacheRegionFactory</property>
<property name="hibernate.cache.use_query_cache">true</property>
```

```

###### Using Second-Level Caching

```java

EntityManager em =
emf.createEntityManager();

User user1 = em.find(User.class, 1L); //
Loaded from second-level cache

User user2 = em.find(User.class, 1L); // Again
from second-level cache

```

3. **Query Caching**

Query Caching is a technique that stores query results to avoid repeated queries to the database. This can be particularly useful for complex or frequently executed queries.
```

Configuring Query Caching

Use `@Query` and `@Cache` to configure query caching:

```java
import javax.persistence.Cacheable;

import javax.persistence.Entity;

import javax.persistence.Id;

import javax.persistence.NamedQuery;


@Entity

@Cacheable

@NamedQuery(name = "User.findAll", query = "SELECT u FROM User u")

public class User {


    @Id

    private Long id;
```

```
    private String name;

    // Constructors, getters, and setters
}
```

Executing the Query with Caching

```java
EntityManager em = emf.createEntityManager();
Query query = em.createNamedQuery("User.findAll");
List<User> users = query.getResultList(); // Results stored in cache
```

Batch Processing

Batch Processing is a technique for optimizing the insertion, updating, and removal of a large number of entities in a single operation. This approach reduces the number of round-trips between the application and the database and can significantly improve performance.

1. **Batch Processing with JPA**

Batch Processing can be achieved using JPA APIs to perform batch operations on multiple entities. Specific implementations may vary depending on the persistence provider.

Example of Batch Processing with Hibernate

Configure Hibernate to use batch processing:

```xml
<property
```

```
name="hibernate.jdbc.batch_size">20</prope
rty>
```

Using Batch Processing

```java
import javax.persistence.EntityManager;

import
javax.persistence.EntityManagerFactory;

import javax.persistence.Persistence;


public class BatchProcessingExample {


    public static void main(String[] args) {

        EntityManagerFactory emf =
Persistence.createEntityManagerFactory("my
PersistenceUnit");

        EntityManager em =
emf.createEntityManager();
```

```
em.getTransaction().begin();

for (int i = 0; i < 100; i++) {
    User user = new User((long) i, "User"
+ i);
    em.persist(user);

    // Execute batch every 20 operations
    if (i % 20 == 0) {
        em.flush();
        em.clear();
    }
}

em.getTransaction().commit();
em.close();
emf.close();
```

    }

}

```

##### Code Explanation

1. **Batch Size Configuration**: Set the `hibernate.jdbc.batch_size` property to specify the number of batch operations to execute at once.

2. **Flush and Clear**: Use `em.flush()` and `em.clear()` to manage memory and ensure that the batch is sent to the database regularly. This helps avoid the accumulation of unmanaged entities in the persistence context cache.

#### 2. **Batch Processing with Standard JPA**
```

Standard JPA does not directly provide a batch processing API, but JPA implementations like Hibernate and EclipseLink offer extensions to handle batch processing.

Performance optimization in JPA requires a balanced approach among different strategies. **Lazy Loading** and **Eager Loading** should be used carefully to avoid performance issues like the N+1 Select Problem and memory overload. **Entity Caching** and query caching can significantly reduce the number of database queries and improve application responsiveness. Finally, **Batch Processing** is essential for efficiently handling large volumes of data.

Understanding and implementing these optimization techniques help ensure that JPA-based applications are scalable, responsive, and capable of efficiently handling data persistence operations. Proper planning and management of these techniques can lead to significant performance improvements and a better user experience.

8.JPA 2.0 and Inheritance

Inheritance is a fundamental concept in object-oriented programming that allows for the creation of a class hierarchy. JPA (Java Persistence API) 2.0 handles inheritance through various mapping strategies that determine how parent and child classes and their properties are persisted in the database. Understanding JPA's inheritance strategies is crucial for designing effective database schemas and maintaining data consistency.

In JPA 2.0, there are three main inheritance strategies for mapping inherited classes and their relationships in the database:

1. **Single Table**

2. **Joined**

3. **Table per Class**

Each strategy has its advantages and

disadvantages, and the choice depends on the specific needs of the application, performance considerations, and maintainability. This guide will explore each of these strategies in detail, providing practical examples and in-depth explanations.

1. Single Table

The **Single Table** strategy is the simplest and most common for handling inheritance in JPA. With this strategy, all classes in the inheritance hierarchy are mapped to a single table in the database. The table contains columns for all properties of both the base and derived classes, and a discriminator column to differentiate between different types of entities.

1.1. **Defining the Single Table Strategy**

To use the Single Table strategy, the

`@Inheritance` annotation with `InheritanceType.SINGLE_TABLE` is used. Additionally, the `@DiscriminatorColumn` annotation is specified to define the column used to distinguish between different entity types.

Example of Single Table Mapping

Consider a class hierarchy with `Animal` as the base class and `Dog` and `Cat` as derived classes.

```java
import javax.persistence.Entity;

import javax.persistence.Id;

import javax.persistence.Inheritance;

import javax.persistence.InheritanceType;

import javax.persistence.DiscriminatorColumn;

import javax.persistence.DiscriminatorValue;
```

```
@Entity
@Inheritance(strategy = InheritanceType.SINGLE_TABLE)
@DiscriminatorColumn(name = "animal_type")
public abstract class Animal {

    @Id
    private Long id;
    private String name;

    // Constructors, getters, and setters
}
```

```java
import javax.persistence.DiscriminatorValue;
import javax.persistence.Entity;
```

```
@Entity
@DiscriminatorValue("DOG")
public class Dog extends Animal {

    private String breed;

    // Constructors, getters, and setters
}
```

```java
import javax.persistence.DiscriminatorValue;
import javax.persistence.Entity;

@Entity
@DiscriminatorValue("CAT")
public class Cat extends Animal {
```

    private String color;

    // Constructors, getters, and setters
}
```

##### Table Schema

The resulting table in the database might have the following schema:

```sql
CREATE TABLE Animal (
    id BIGINT PRIMARY KEY,
    name VARCHAR(255),
    animal_type VARCHAR(31), -- Discriminator column
    breed VARCHAR(255),      -- Column for

Dog

    color VARCHAR(255)       -- Column for Cat

);

```

Advantages and Disadvantages

Advantages:

- Simplicity of implementation.

- Minimal number of joins needed during queries.

Disadvantages:

- The table can become very large and contain many unused columns, reducing space efficiency and performance.

- May be less suitable for complex inheritance hierarchies or hierarchies with many derived classes.
```

2. Joined

The **Joined** strategy creates a table for each class in the inheritance hierarchy. The base class table contains columns for the properties of the base class, while the derived class tables contain only columns specific to their properties. The derived class tables have a foreign key that references the base class table.

2.1. **Defining the Joined Strategy**

To use the Joined strategy, the `@Inheritance` annotation with `InheritanceType.JOINED` is used.

Example of Joined Mapping

Using the same class hierarchy of `Animal`, `Dog`, and `Cat`.

```java
import javax.persistence.Entity;

import javax.persistence.Id;

import javax.persistence.Inheritance;

import javax.persistence.InheritanceType;


@Entity

@Inheritance(strategy =
InheritanceType.JOINED)

public abstract class Animal {


    @Id

    private Long id;

    private String name;


    // Constructors, getters, and setters

}
```

```

```java
import javax.persistence.Entity;

@Entity
public class Dog extends Animal {

    private String breed;

    // Constructors, getters, and setters
}
```

```java
import javax.persistence.Entity;

@Entity

public class Cat extends Animal {

    private String color;

    // Constructors, getters, and setters
}
```

Table Schemas

The resulting tables in the database might have the following schema:

```sql
CREATE TABLE Animal (
    id BIGINT PRIMARY KEY,
    name VARCHAR(255)
);

```
CREATE TABLE Dog (
    id BIGINT PRIMARY KEY,
    breed VARCHAR(255),
    CONSTRAINT FK_Dog_Animal FOREIGN KEY (id) REFERENCES Animal(id)
);

CREATE TABLE Cat (
    id BIGINT PRIMARY KEY,
    color VARCHAR(255),
    CONSTRAINT FK_Cat_Animal FOREIGN KEY (id) REFERENCES Animal(id)
);
```

Advantages and Disadvantages

Advantages:

- The base class table is smaller and more manageable, containing only common columns.

- Derived class tables contain only specific columns, reducing the spread of null data.

Disadvantages:

- Greater query complexity due to joins between tables.

- Potential performance impact due to the need to execute joins during read and write operations.

3. Table per Class

The **Table per Class** strategy creates a separate table for each class in the inheritance hierarchy, including all columns of both the base class and the derived classes. Each table fully represents a single class.

3.1. **Defining the Table per Class Strategy**

To use the Table per Class strategy, the `@Inheritance` annotation with `InheritanceType.TABLE_PER_CLASS` is used.

Example of Table per Class Mapping

Using the same class hierarchy of `Animal`, `Dog`, and `Cat`.

```java
import javax.persistence.Entity;

import javax.persistence.Id;

import javax.persistence.Inheritance;

import javax.persistence.InheritanceType;
```

```
@Entity
@Inheritance(strategy = InheritanceType.TABLE_PER_CLASS)
public abstract class Animal {

    @Id
    private Long id;
    private String name;

    // Constructors, getters, and setters
}
```

```java
import javax.persistence.Entity;

@Entity
```

```
public class Dog extends Animal {

    private String breed;

    // Constructors, getters, and setters
}
```

```java
import javax.persistence.Entity;

@Entity
public class Cat extends Animal {

    private String color;

    // Constructors, getters, and setters
}
```

```

##### Table Schemas

The resulting tables in the database might have the following schema:

```sql
CREATE TABLE Animal (
   id BIGINT PRIMARY KEY,
   name VARCHAR(255)
);

CREATE TABLE Dog (
   id BIGINT PRIMARY KEY,
   name VARCHAR(255),
   breed VARCHAR(255)
);

```
CREATE TABLE Cat (
   id BIGINT PRIMARY KEY,
   name VARCHAR(255),
   color VARCHAR(255)
);
```

Advantages and Disadvantages

Advantages:

- Each table is fully autonomous and represents a single class.

- No joins are needed to retrieve data for a single class, reducing query complexity.

Disadvantages:

- Duplication of columns in the base class table can cause redundancy and inefficiency.

- May be less efficient in terms of space and performance compared to other strategies.

Conclusion

Choosing the right inheritance strategy in JPA depends on the specific needs of the application and the database design.

- **Single Table** is simple and efficient for straightforward inheritance hierarchies but can become inefficient for complex hierarchies due to many scattered columns and potential null data.

- **Joined** offers good normalization and a clear representation of hierarchies but can introduce query complexity and performance impact due to the necessary joins.

- **Table per Class** ensures clear table separation but may lead to inefficiencies and data duplication.

It is crucial to carefully consider the trade-offs between simplicity, performance, and maintainability when deciding which strategy to use. The right choice will depend on the specific needs of the application and the characteristics of the domain model.

9.Integration of JPA with Other Frameworks

Integrating JPA (Java Persistence API) with other frameworks is crucial for fully leveraging data persistence capabilities and enhancing application development efficiency. JPA can be combined with various frameworks, each offering specific functionalities and advantages. In this section, we will explore how JPA integrates with **Spring**, **Java EE**, and **Hibernate**, providing details and practical examples for each case.

JPA and Spring

Spring is a popular framework that supports modular and configurable Java application development. Integrating JPA with Spring simplifies transaction management, data access, and repository configuration.

1. Configuring JPA with Spring

To integrate JPA with Spring, you need to configure an `EntityManagerFactory` and a `TransactionManager` so that Spring can manage the lifecycle of entities and transactions.

1.1. Configuring Spring with JPA

1.1.1. Configuration via XML

In the `applicationContext.xml` file, configure the `EntityManagerFactory` and `TransactionManager`:

```xml
<beans
xmlns="http://www.springframework.org/sch
ema/beans"
```

```
xmlns:xsi="http://www.w3.org/2001/XMLSc
hema-instance"

xsi:schemaLocation="http://www.springframe
work.org/schema/beans

http://www.springframework.org/schema/bean
s/spring-beans.xsd">


  <!-- DataSource Configuration -->

  <bean id="dataSource"
class="org.springframework.jdbc.datasource.
DriverManagerDataSource">

      <property name="driverClassName"
value="com.mysql.cj.jdbc.Driver" />

      <property name="url"
value="jdbc:mysql://localhost:3306/mydb" />

      <property name="username"
value="root" />

      <property name="password"
value="password" />

  </bean>
```

```
    <!-- EntityManagerFactory Configuration
-->
    <bean id="entityManagerFactory"

class="org.springframework.orm.jpa.LocalCo
ntainerEntityManagerFactoryBean">
        <property name="dataSource"
ref="dataSource" />
        <property name="persistenceUnitName"
value="myPersistenceUnit" />
        <property name="jpaVendorAdapter">
            <bean
class="org.springframework.orm.jpa.vendor.H
ibernateJpaVendorAdapter">
                <property name="showSql"
value="true" />
                <property name="generateDdl"
value="true" />
            </bean>
        </property>
```

```
    </bean>

    <!-- TransactionManager Configuration -->
    <bean id="transactionManager"
class="org.springframework.orm.jpa.JpaTransactionManager">
        <property name="entityManagerFactory" ref="entityManagerFactory" />
    </bean>

    <!-- Enable Transaction Management -->
    <tx:annotation-driven transaction-manager="transactionManager" />
</beans>
```

1.1.2. Configuration via Java Config

Alternatively, you can use Java-based configuration:

```java
import org.springframework.context.annotation.Bean;

import org.springframework.context.annotation.Configuration;

import org.springframework.data.jpa.repository.config.EnableJpaRepositories;

import org.springframework.orm.jpa.JpaTransactionManager;

import org.springframework.orm.jpa.LocalContainerEntityManagerFactoryBean;

import org.springframework.transaction.PlatformTransactionManager;

import org.springframework.transaction.annotation.E
```

```
nableTransactionManagement;


import
javax.persistence.EntityManagerFactory;
import javax.sql.DataSource;
import
org.springframework.jdbc.datasource.DriverM
anagerDataSource;


@Configuration
@EnableTransactionManagement
@EnableJpaRepositories(basePackages =
"com.example.repository")
public class JpaConfig {


   @Bean
   public DataSource dataSource() {
      DriverManagerDataSource dataSource =
new DriverManagerDataSource();
```

```
dataSource.setDriverClassName("com.mysql.
cj.jdbc.Driver");

dataSource.setUrl("jdbc:mysql://localhost:330
6/mydb");
        dataSource.setUsername("root");
        dataSource.setPassword("password");
        return dataSource;
    }

    @Bean
    public
LocalContainerEntityManagerFactoryBean
entityManagerFactory(DataSource
dataSource) {

LocalContainerEntityManagerFactoryBean
emf = new
LocalContainerEntityManagerFactoryBean();
        emf.setDataSource(dataSource);
```

```
emf.setPersistenceUnitName("myPersistence
Unit");

emf.setPackagesToScan("com.example.entity
");
        // JPA Vendor Adapter Configuration
        return emf;
    }

    @Bean
    public PlatformTransactionManager
transactionManager(EntityManagerFactory
emf) {
        JpaTransactionManager
transactionManager = new
JpaTransactionManager();

transactionManager.setEntityManagerFactory(
emf);
        return transactionManager;
    }
```

```
}
```

1.2. Using Spring Data JPA Repositories

Spring Data JPA simplifies data access by creating repositories that extend `JpaRepository` or `CrudRepository`. Here is an example of defining a repository:

```java
import org.springframework.data.jpa.repository.JpaRepository;
import com.example.entity.User;

public interface UserRepository extends JpaRepository<User, Long> {
    User findByUsername(String username);
```

}
```

##### 1.3. Using the Repository

```java
import
org.springframework.beans.factory.annotation
.Autowired;
import
org.springframework.stereotype.Service;

@Service
public class UserService {

    @Autowired
    private UserRepository userRepository;

    public User findUserByUsername(String

```
username) {
      return
userRepository.findByUsername(username);
   }
}
```

Advantages of Integrating JPA with Spring:

- **Automatic Transaction Management**: Spring automatically handles transactions via annotations.

- **Simplified Configuration**: Configuration is centralized and can be done via XML or Java.

- **Repository Support**: Spring Data JPA repositories simplify CRUD operations and custom queries.

JPA and Java EE

Java EE (Java Platform, Enterprise Edition), now known as Jakarta EE, is a platform for developing enterprise Java applications. JPA is a core component of Java EE, providing persistence APIs for managing entities and transactions.

2. Configuring JPA in a Java EE Environment

In Java EE, JPA is configured via the `persistence.xml` file and integrated with the Java EE application server.

2.1. Configuring `persistence.xml`

The `persistence.xml` file is used to configure persistence units and the JPA provider. It is located in the `META-INF` directory.

```xml
```

```
<persistence
xmlns="http://xmlns.jcp.org/xml/ns/persistenc
e"

xmlns:xsi="http://www.w3.org/2001/XMLSc
hema-instance"

xsi:schemaLocation="http://xmlns.jcp.org/xml
/ns/persistence

http://xmlns.jcp.org/xml/ns/persistence/persist
ence_2_1.xsd"
          version="2.1">
   <persistence-unit
name="myPersistenceUnit">

<provider>org.hibernate.jpa.HibernatePersiste
nceProvider</provider>
      <class>com.example.entity.User</class>
      <!-- Database Connection Configuration
-->
      <properties>
```

```
        <property
name="javax.persistence.jdbc.driver"
value="com.mysql.cj.jdbc.Driver"/>

        <property
name="javax.persistence.jdbc.url"
value="jdbc:mysql://localhost:3306/mydb"/>

        <property
name="javax.persistence.jdbc.user"
value="root"/>

        <property
name="javax.persistence.jdbc.password"
value="password"/>

        <property name="hibernate.dialect"
value="org.hibernate.dialect.MySQL5Dialect"
/>

        <property
name="hibernate.hbm2ddl.auto"
value="update"/>

      </properties>

   </persistence-unit>

</persistence>
```

2.2. Injecting EntityManager

In a Java EE environment, the `EntityManager` can be injected directly into EJBs or servlets. Here is an example of using it in an EJB:

```java
import javax.ejb.Stateless;

import javax.inject.Inject;

import javax.persistence.EntityManager;

import javax.persistence.PersistenceContext;


@Stateless

public class UserService {


    @PersistenceContext(unitName = "myPersistenceUnit")
```

```
    private EntityManager em;

    public User findUserById(Long id) {
        return em.find(User.class, id);
    }

    public void createUser(User user) {
        em.persist(user);
    }
}
```

2.3. Using CDI (Contexts and Dependency Injection)

In a Java EE application, you can use CDI to manage object dependencies and inject `EntityManager`:

```java
import javax.inject.Inject;
import javax.transaction.Transactional;

@Transactional
public class UserService {

    @Inject
    private EntityManager em;

    public User findUserById(Long id) {
        return em.find(User.class, id);
    }

    public void createUser(User user) {
        em.persist(user);
    }
}
```

```

**Advantages of Integrating JPA with Java EE**:

- **Native Integration**: JPA is a core part of Java EE, so no additional configuration is needed for the persistence provider.

- **Support for EJB and CDI**: Direct use of EJB and CDI for managing entities and transactions.

- **Automatic Transaction Management**: Java EE handles transactions automatically.

### JPA with Hibernate

**Hibernate** is one of the most popular and advanced implementations of JPA. Providing a comprehensive JPA implementation, Hibernate also offers additional features such as advanced caching, batch processing, and a powerful Criteria API.
```

3. Configuring JPA with Hibernate

Hibernate can be used as a JPA provider by configuring it in the `persistence.xml` file or using Java-based configuration.

3.1. Configuring Hibernate via `persistence.xml`

Here is an example of configuring Hibernate in the `persistence.xml` file:

```xml
<persistence
xmlns="http://xmlns.jcp.org/xml/ns/persistence"

xmlns:xsi="http://www.w3.org/2001/XMLSchema-instance"

xsi:schemaLocation="http://xmlns.jcp.org/xml
```

```
/ns/persistence

http://xmlns.jcp.org/xml/ns/persistence/persist
ence_2_1.xsd"

        version="2.1">

   <persistence-unit
name="myPersistenceUnit">

<provider>org.hibernate.jpa.HibernatePersiste
nceProvider</

provider>

      <class>com.example.entity.User</class>

      <!-- Database Connection Configuration
-->

      <properties>

         <property
name="javax.persistence.jdbc.driver"
value="com.mysql.cj.jdbc.Driver"/>

         <property
name="javax.persistence.jdbc.url"
```

```
value="jdbc:mysql://localhost:3306/mydb"/>

        <property
name="javax.persistence.jdbc.user"
value="root"/>

        <property
name="javax.persistence.jdbc.password"
value="password"/>

        <property name="hibernate.dialect"
value="org.hibernate.dialect.MySQL5Dialect"
/>

        <property
name="hibernate.hbm2ddl.auto"
value="update"/>

        <property name="hibernate.show_sql"
value="true"/>

        <property
name="hibernate.format_sql" value="true"/>

      </properties>

   </persistence-unit>

</persistence>
```

3.2. Configuring Hibernate via Java Config

Using Java configuration, you can configure Hibernate as follows:

```java
import org.springframework.context.annotation.Bean;

import org.springframework.context.annotation.Configuration;

import org.springframework.orm.jpa.JpaTransactionManager;

import org.springframework.orm.jpa.LocalContainerEntityManagerFactoryBean;

import org.springframework.orm.jpa.vendor.HibernateJpaVendorAdapter;
```

```
import
org.springframework.transaction.PlatformTra
nsactionManager;

import
javax.persistence.EntityManagerFactory;

import javax.sql.DataSource;

import
org.springframework.jdbc.datasource.DriverM
anagerDataSource;


@Configuration

public class HibernateConfig {


   @Bean

   public DataSource dataSource() {

      DriverManagerDataSource dataSource =
new DriverManagerDataSource();


dataSource.setDriverClassName("com.mysql.
cj.jdbc.Driver");
```

```
dataSource.setUrl("jdbc:mysql://localhost:330
6/mydb");
        dataSource.setUsername("root");
        dataSource.setPassword("password");
        return dataSource;
    }

    @Bean
    public
LocalContainerEntityManagerFactoryBean
entityManagerFactory(DataSource
dataSource) {

LocalContainerEntityManagerFactoryBean
emf = new
LocalContainerEntityManagerFactoryBean();
        emf.setDataSource(dataSource);

emf.setPackagesToScan("com.example.entity
");
        HibernateJpaVendorAdapter adapter =
```

```
new HibernateJpaVendorAdapter();
        adapter.setShowSql(true);
        adapter.setGenerateDdl(true);
        emf.setJpaVendorAdapter(adapter);
        return emf;
    }

    @Bean
    public PlatformTransactionManager transactionManager(EntityManagerFactory emf) {
        return new JpaTransactionManager(emf);
    }
}
```

3.3. Using Advanced Hibernate Features

Hibernate offers numerous advanced features such as caching and batch processing that can be configured via Hibernate properties.

Example of configuring second-level caching:

```xml
<property name="hibernate.cache.use_second_level_cache" value="true"/>

<property name="hibernate.cache.region.factory_class" value="org.hibernate.cache.ehcache.EhCacheRegionFactory"/>
```

Example of configuring batch processing:

```xml
```

```
<property name="hibernate.jdbc.batch_size" value="20"/>
```

Example of using Hibernate Criteria API:

```java
import javax.persistence.CriteriaBuilder;
import javax.persistence.CriteriaQuery;
import javax.persistence.EntityManager;
import javax.persistence.PersistenceContext;
import javax.persistence.TypedQuery;
import java.util.List;

public class UserService {

    @PersistenceContext
    private EntityManager em;
```

```
    public List<User> findUsersWithCriteria(String name) {
        CriteriaBuilder cb = em.getCriteriaBuilder();
        CriteriaQuery<User> cq = cb.createQuery(User.class);
        var root = cq.from(User.class);

        cq.select(root).where(cb.equal(root.get("name"), name));
        TypedQuery<User> query = em.createQuery(cq);
        return query.getResultList();
    }
}
```

Advantages of Integrating JPA with Hibernate:

- **Advanced Features**: Hibernate offers advanced features such as second-level caching and batch processing.

- **Full JPA Support**: Hibernate provides a complete implementation of JPA and supports all JPA specifications.

- **Flexible Configuration**: Configurations can be done via XML or Java, depending on preferences and needs.

Integrating JPA with **Spring**, **Java EE**, and **Hibernate** provides a wide range of options for managing data persistence in Java applications.

- **JPA and Spring** offer simplified configuration and advanced transaction management through Spring Data JPA repositories.

- **JPA and Java EE** provide native integration with Java EE containers and direct support for transactions and `EntityManager` injection.

- **JPA with Hibernate** delivers a powerful JPA implementation with advanced features such as caching and batch processing.

Choosing the right framework for JPA integration depends on the specific needs of the application, project characteristics, and the development team's preferences. With proper configuration and a thorough understanding of the features offered, it's possible to build scalable, efficient, and maintainable Java applications.

10.Troubleshooting Common Issues in JPA

When working with JPA (Java Persistence API), encountering common issues that can affect application functionality is inevitable. Troubleshooting these issues requires a deep understanding of JPA, debugging techniques, and performance optimization strategies. In this article, we will explore common errors in JPA, debugging techniques, and performance tuning strategies, providing details and practical examples to address each area.

Common JPA Errors

Errors in JPA can range from configuration issues to runtime errors related to entity and transaction management. Here’s a list of common errors and their solutions.

1. Configuration Errors

1.1. `PersistenceException`: `persistence.xml` Configuration Issues

A common error involves incorrect configuration of the `persistence.xml` file, which can lead to a `PersistenceException` during application startup. Typical errors include:

- **Missing or Incorrect `persistence.xml` File**:

  Ensure that the `persistence.xml` file is present in the `META-INF` folder and is correctly formatted. Here is an example of a correct configuration:

```xml
  <persistence
xmlns="http://xmlns.jcp.org/xml/ns/persistence"

xmlns:xsi="http://www.w3.org/2001/XMLSchema-instance"
```

```
xsi:schemaLocation="http://xmlns.jcp.org/xml
/ns/persistence

http://xmlns.jcp.org/xml/ns/persistence/persist
ence_2_1.xsd"

           version="2.1">

    <persistence-unit
name="myPersistenceUnit">

<provider>org.hibernate.jpa.HibernatePersiste
nceProvider</provider>

<class>com.example.entity.User</class>

        <properties>

            <property
name="javax.persistence.jdbc.driver"
value="com.mysql.cj.jdbc.Driver"/>

            <property
name="javax.persistence.jdbc.url"
value="jdbc:mysql://localhost:3306/mydb"/>

            <property
name="javax.persistence.jdbc.user"
```

```
value="root"/>

          <property
name="javax.persistence.jdbc.password"
value="password"/>

          <property name="hibernate.dialect"
value="org.hibernate.dialect.MySQL5Dialect"
/>

        </properties>

     </persistence-unit>

  </persistence>
```

- **Incorrect Persistence Unit Name**:

  Make sure that the persistence unit name specified in `persistence.xml` matches the one used in your code.

1.2. `NoPersistenceProviderFoundException`: No Persistence Provider Found

This error indicates that no persistence provider was found in the classpath. Verify that the JPA provider is included in your project's dependencies. For example, if you are using Hibernate, ensure that you have the correct dependency:

```xml
<dependency>
    <groupId>org.hibernate</groupId>
    <artifactId>hibernate-core</artifactId>
    <version>5.6.10.Final</version>
</dependency>
```

2. Runtime Errors

2.1. `EntityNotFoundException`: Entity Not Found

This error occurs when trying to access an entity that does not exist in the database. Ensure that the entity ID is correct and that the entity exists in the database. Example of safe entity access:

```java
public User findUserById(Long id) {
    User user = em.find(User.class, id);
    if (user == null) {
        throw new EntityNotFoundException("User with ID " + id + " not found");
    }
    return user;
}
```

2.2. `OptimisticLockException`: Optimistic Locking Conflict

This error indicates that there was a conflict when updating an entity due to simultaneous modifications. Ensure that you handle optimistic locking conflicts using the entity version. Example:

```java
@Entity
public class User {

    @Id
    @GeneratedValue(strategy = GenerationType.IDENTITY)
    private Long id;

    @Version
    private Integer version;

    // other fields and methods
```

}

```

**2.3. `TransactionRequiredException`: Transaction Required**

This error occurs when attempting to perform a persistence operation without an active transaction. Ensure that all persistence operations are executed within a transaction. Example of transaction management using annotations:

```java
@Transactional
public void createUser(User user) {
    em.persist(user);
}
```
```

Debugging Techniques

Debugging JPA applications can be complex, but there are several techniques and tools that can help identify and resolve issues.

1. Enabling SQL Query Logging

Enabling SQL query logging can provide valuable insights into what is happening at the database level. With Hibernate, you can enable SQL query logging by adding the following properties:

```xml
<property name="hibernate.show_sql"
value="true"/>

<property name="hibernate.format_sql"
value="true"/>
```

This will display all SQL queries generated by Hibernate in the console.

2. Using Logging

Set the logging level for Hibernate and JPA to get detailed information. For example, to log all executed queries, you can configure logging in `log4j` or `logback`:

Example of logback configuration:

```xml
<configuration>
   <appender name="STDOUT" class="ch.qos.logback.core.ConsoleAppender">
       <encoder>
           <pattern>%d{yyyy-MM-dd HH:mm:ss} %-5level %logger{36} - %msg %n</pattern>
```

```
        </encoder>
    </appender>

    <logger name="org.hibernate.SQL" level="DEBUG"/>
    <logger name="org.hibernate.type.descriptor.sql.BasicBinder" level="TRACE"/>

    <root level="INFO">
        <appender-ref ref="STDOUT"/>
    </root>
</configuration>
```

3. Using Profiling Tools

Profiling tools such as **JProfiler** or **VisualVM** can help identify performance issues and bottlenecks in JPA queries. These tools allow you to examine SQL queries, monitor method calls, and analyze memory usage.

4. Debugging Transactions

To diagnose transaction issues, it's useful to examine the transaction logs and check if transactions are being managed correctly. Ensure that all persistence operations are wrapped in a transaction, especially when using manual transactions.

Performance Tuning

Optimizing JPA application performance requires a combination of correct configuration, caching techniques, and efficient fetching strategies.

1. Lazy and Eager Loading

1.1. Lazy Loading

Lazy loading is a fetching strategy that loads data only when it is actually needed. This is the default strategy for collections and `@ManyToOne` and `@OneToOne` associations. Here’s an example:

```java
@Entity
public class Order {

    @Id
    @GeneratedValue(strategy = GenerationType.IDENTITY)
    private Long id;

    @ManyToOne(fetch = FetchType.LAZY)
    private Customer customer;
```

    // other fields and methods

}

```

The `fetch = FetchType.LAZY` indicates that the `Customer` entity will be loaded only when accessed.

**1.2. Eager Loading**

**Eager loading** loads associated data along with the main entity. This can be useful when you know you will need the associations immediately. Here’s an example:

```java

@Entity

public class Order {

```
    @Id
    @GeneratedValue(strategy = GenerationType.IDENTITY)
    private Long id;

    @ManyToOne(fetch = FetchType.EAGER)
    private Customer customer;

    // other fields and methods
}
```

Use `eager loading` cautiously as it can lead to performance issues and unnecessary data fetching.

2. Entity Caching

Caching can significantly improve JPA

application performance by reducing database access. There are two levels of caching in JPA:

2.1. First-Level Caching

First-level caching is automatically managed by JPA through the `EntityManager`. Each `EntityManager` maintains a cache of entity data it manages during the session's lifetime.

2.2. Second-Level Caching

Second-level caching is managed by Hibernate and needs to be explicitly configured. You can configure second-level caching using Ehcache or other caching solutions. Here’s an example with Ehcache:

```xml
<property
```

```
name="hibernate.cache.use_second_level_cache" value="true"/>

<property
name="hibernate.cache.region.factory_class"
value="org.hibernate.cache.ehcache.EhCacheRegionFactory"/>
```

Example of Ehcache configuration:

```xml
<ehcache>

  <cache name="com.example.entity.User"

        maxEntries="1000"

        eternal="false"

        timeToIdleSeconds="3600"

        timeToLiveSeconds="7200"

        overflowToDisk="true"

        maxElementsOnDisk="10000"/>
```

```
</ehcache>
```

3. Batch Processing

Batch processing can enhance the performance of batch persistence operations by reducing the number of round-trips to the database. You can configure batch processing in Hibernate by adding the following properties:

```xml
<property name="hibernate.jdbc.batch_size" value="20"/>
```

This example configures Hibernate to perform 20 insert operations in a batch.

Example of batch processing in code:

```java
@Transactional
public void batchInsertUsers(List<User> users) {
    int batchSize = 20;
    for (int i = 0; i < users.size(); i++) {
        em.persist(users.get(i));
        if (i % batchSize == 0 && i > 0) {
            em.flush();
            em.clear();
        }
    }
}
```

Troubleshooting common JPA issues, debugging, and performance optimization are crucial for developing robust and efficient Java applications. Understanding common errors, applying effective debugging techniques, and using performance optimization strategies such as lazy/eager loading, caching, and batch processing can significantly enhance the reliability and performance of your JPA applications.

Adopting best practices and using the right tools can make a big difference in the quality and efficiency of your code, making your application more scalable and maintainable.

Index

www.ingramcontent.com/pod-product-compliance
Lightning Source LLC
Chambersburg PA
CBHW052149220526
45471CB00004B/1592
* 9 7 9 8 3 3 6 6 5 0 2 4 2 *